Astral Projection

Unlocking the Secrets of Astral Travel and Having a Willful Out-of-Body Experience, Including Tips for Entering the Astral Plane and Shifting into Higher Consciousness

© **Copyright 2018**

All Rights Reserved. No part of this book may be reproduced in any form without permission in writing from the author. Reviewers may quote brief passages in reviews.

Disclaimer: No part of this publication may be reproduced or transmitted in any form or by any means, mechanical or electronic, including photocopying or recording, or by any information storage and retrieval system, or transmitted by email without permission in writing from the publisher.

While all attempts have been made to verify the information provided in this publication, neither the author nor the publisher assumes any responsibility for errors, omissions or contrary interpretations of the subject matter herein.

This book is for entertainment purposes only. The views expressed are those of the author alone, and should not be taken as expert instruction or commands. The reader is responsible for his or her own actions.

Adherence to all applicable laws and regulations, including international, federal, state and local laws governing professional licensing, business practices, advertising and all other aspects of doing business in the US, Canada, UK or any other jurisdiction is the sole responsibility of the purchaser or reader.

Neither the author nor the publisher assumes any responsibility or liability whatsoever on the behalf of the purchaser or reader of these materials. Any perceived slight of any individual or organization is purely unintentional.

Contents

INTRODUCTION 1
CHAPTER 1: WHAT IS ASTRAL PROJECTION? 2
CHAPTER 2: WHAT TO KNOW BEFORE YOU TRY ASTRAL PROJECTION AND WHAT MIGHT BE HOLDING YOU BACK 7
EAT 7
    HYDRATE 8
    MEDITATE 8
    VISUALIZE 10
    FEAR 10
    DOUBT 11
CHAPTER 3: BEST ASTRAL PROJECTION TECHNIQUES AND HOW TO PERFORM THEM 12
    SPACE 12
    BREATHE 14
    MEDITATE 15
    VIBRATIONAL STAGE 16
    VISUALIZE MOVEMENT 17

ASTRAL PROJECTION 18

CHAPTER 4: HOW DO I COME BACK AND WHAT TO DO AFTER?....24

CHAPTER 5: WHAT IS THE DOWNSIDE OF ASTRAL PROJECTION? 28

ONE 28

ANOTHER 29

LUCID DREAMING 30

CHAPTER 6: FREQUENTLY ASKED QUESTIONS ABOUT ASTRAL PROJECTION 32

HOW MUCH TIME DOES IT TAKE TO ASTRAL PROJECT? 32

DO I NEED TO PROTECT MYSELF IN ANY WAY? 33

HOW DO I KNOW IF IT WORKED? 33

AM I CRAZY TO BELIEVE IN ASTRAL PROJECTION? 34

I HAVEN'T BEEN ABLE TO ACHIEVE ASTRAL PROJECTION—WHAT CAN I DO? 34

IS IT POSSIBLE TO SWITCH BODIES WITH SOMEONE ELSE? 35

ARE THERE ANY DRUGS OR SUBSTANCES I CAN TAKE TO HELP WITH ASTRAL PROJECTION? 36

ARE NEAR-DEATH EXPERIENCES A TYPE OF ASTRAL PROJECTION? 36

WHEN IS THE BEST TIME TO ASTRAL PROJECT? 36

CONCLUSION 38

Introduction

In this book, you will learn the basics of the ancient concept of astral projection, or "Out-of-Body Experience," in which a person willfully leaves their body. That is to say that the consciousness, or astral body, is capable of leaving the physical body and can actually move around as a separate entity. As human beings, we have the ability to initiate and control this experience (that is why the word "willful" is so important—this is a voluntary experience). All that is required is an open mind and the willingness to learn—to put aside what we think we know to allow ourselves to experience a higher degree of consciousness.

The following chapters will discuss what exactly astral projection is, what you should know before trying it, how to have the best possible experience, what may be keeping you from entering the astral plane, the downsides of astral projection, and Frequently Asked Questions. The goal is to help make sure you get all the knowledge you need before starting the fascinating practice of astral projection!

Chapter 1: What Is Astral Projection?

Before we can get started with astral projection, it is, of course, necessary to know just what exactly astral projection is. A good definition that we will use here, is that astral projection is a purposeful, spiritual out-of-body experience. That is to say, a person's astral body separates from the physical body. The person experiencing the astral projection is aware of and involved with what is happening.

Humans have been interested in the separation of mind and body since the beginning of time. It has been mentioned by civilizations including ancient Egypt, China, India, and Amazon tribes. The idea that we can experience such unknown concepts has certainly captured our imagination. Science fiction has always been a popular topic in literature, television, and movies. Paranormal interests are a normal and fascinating topic for people.

The attraction of astral projection is obvious. While we experience and interact with the physical world and its inhabitants every day, the idea of a spiritual, unknown, energetic world—located just beyond a divide but still accessible by human beings—has an irresistible appeal. People are inherently explorers, travelers, and adventurers, after all. This makes the idea of humanity exploring the unknown as old as the story of humanity itself.

The astral body can be considered the liaison between the spirit or soul and the physical body. It is the animated, spiritual component of the human consciousness, part of the soul yet capable of separating. It is due to this unique status that people are able to travel outside their bodies. The soul is incapable of leaving the bod, as without it, the person would die. This also makes astral projection different from near-death experiences, which occur when the soul *actually* leaves the body for a short time. Near-death experiences are also involuntary, as opposed to the mindful nature of astral projecting.

It must be considered that these experiences all take place internally and that the astral being and physical body don't *actually* separate. This question cannot be definitively answered, as there can never be a definitive proof of astral projection. There is no way to take photographs during astral projection, for instance. This should not be considered as diminishing to the importance or possibility of traveling out of the body. This practice is very moving and personal to many people, and the knowledge and feelings that they experience are very real.

You will travel through the astral plane, which is also known as the spiritual world. It is a paranormal level of existence beyond what we will ever know in the physical world where we live our day-to-day lives. It is one of the seven planes defined by some as being an elusive area of being. The other six planes are etheric/physical (this is the plane where human life exists), causal/mental, essential, spiritual, monadic, and "manifestal." The astral projections discussed here only involve the astral plane, which is the nearest one to our physical world.

What are some benefits of astral projection? One is spiritual awakening and growth, the knowledge that there is much more to existence than what is present in the physical world. In the astral realm, we can see unimaginable things, meet and interact with other people and beings, move unimpeded through time and space. Similar to how traveling through the world is considered a positive vehicle for personal growth, traveling through the astral world can operate in the same manner. If personal growth on a spiritual level is your goal, then astral projection is a great possibility for you. You will learn that consciousness does not require a physical body to thrive. This can be truly life-altering for many people, as that very idea goes against what we understand about our existence.

Over and over again, people report overwhelmingly positive feelings as a result of astral projection. These include feeling:

- More self-confident
- More appreciative of life
- A sense of inner peace
- Less stress and tension
- More energetic

Most of us would agree that if there were a 'magic pill' that could offer even one of these outcomes, we would be more than happy to take it. In fact, we would probably do everything we could to get our hands on it! That is another way to think of astral projection. It offers its practitioners these benefits in a way that is safe. To repeat, the person is in control the entire time. There really are not any side effects, and certainly nothing questionable or dangerous, like what can be found in some 'magic pills!' And, no prescription is required.

Please always keep in mind that everyone's experiences will be different, just as everyone's experiences in this plane are different. There is enough information that we can surmise what astral projection may be like, but no two people will have the same practice.

You may find that you develop an interest in past lives through your work. Through your spiritual travels and heightened consciousness, you will open yourself up to new avenues of knowledge that you may not have previously had.

Another benefit of astral projection is the friendships you can make with people in the physical 'real' world! On the Internet, there are numerous fan sites, YouTube channels, forums, and other places for people who are interested in and practice astral projection. In a world where social isolation and loneliness are ever increasing, this is an important consideration. When the topic is something that can be misunderstood and controversial, like astral projection, it is even more imperative. The people in your life who do not understand, or maybe even believe in, out-of-body experiences may be dismissive, uninterested or mock your newfound interest, leaving you feeling isolated and alone. Since you are undoubtedly having a great time in the astral realm, it can be disappointing and frustrating to not have people with whom you can share your excitement. Fortunately, you will definitely be able to find likeminded people online who will be encouraging, interested and supportive of your experiences. Lots of times, people who initially meet online decide to meet up in real life, forming deep friendships. You may even decide to visit the astral realm with some of your new friends—why not, when anything is possible! Just think of how much deeper and more intense these experiences will be when shared with other people who are as passionate and excited about it as you are.

Try to be understanding and compassionate toward the people in your life who are not supportive of your interest in the astral realm. It is highly likely that their reaction is based on fear of the unknown, rather than any specific issue with astral projection. It is up to you to understand that their spiritual side is simply not as developed as yours and behave accordingly. It may be easiest to just not talk about it with them, as this will spare both sides from having some uncomfortable and even argumentative situations. It is not your job to educate anyone who is not interested, and it is not anyone else's job to change your mind about your beliefs. It is much easier and more positive to just stay away from the subject with certain people and much better than removing people from your life just because you differ in opinion on this one subject.

If your interest grows, it is extremely likely that you will be able to find classes, whether online or in your community, that can help you to develop your skills and knowledge even more. You are encouraged to take advantage of whatever opportunities you can find to help develop your consciousness. The benefits are too many to mention, and by becoming a better person, you will be doing your part to make the world a better place. Not everyone can say that, but you can and should be proud of that fact.

Please know that astral projection is different from sleep paralysis. That is when the person is in a state of consciousness but is unable to move the body. It only lasts for a few minutes before the person regains control of his body. It is considered a state of being between awake and asleep, so somewhat similar to the hypnagogic state, and most often occurs either when first falling asleep or waking up. The difference here, of course, is that when you are in the hypnagogic state, you are in full control, but in sleep paralysis, it is the opposite result. Sleep paralysis is frightening when it happens, but it is considered to be relatively harmless and no treatment is recommended.

Chapter 2: What to Know Before You Try Astral Projection and What Might Be Holding You Back

Eat

As with any physical and/or mental activity, it is crucial that you prepare yourself physically. The best, easiest, and most effective way of doing this is to eat a proper diet. It is not necessary to go on a special eating plan or anything like that before you start astral projection—but you should definitely be thinking of food as fuel for your body. You should be eating as clean as possible and avoiding packaged and junk food as much as you can. You are going to be asking a lot of your physical self throughout this process and need your body to be as prepared as possible. Without proper nutrition, you may quickly start feeling tired and will lose concentration. Focus on eating fresh fruits and vegetables, lean proteins (stay away from red meat, if possible), whole grains, beans and legumes, and healthy fats. Avoid sugar, caffeine, processed foods, fast food, and alcohol—and organic foods are definitely recommended. Don't eat a big, heavy meal just before astral projection, as digestion can reroute the body's energy away from the task at hand.

Hydrate

Just as important as eating well is drinking enough water. It is essential to keep your body hydrated, as water keeps your body working properly. You would never think of exercising without drinking water, and it can be helpful to think of preparing for astral projection in a similar way. Water regulates all of the body's systems, and without it, we simply don't work in the same way. There are no hard and fast rules that you should drink X number of ounces in a day. It is more important to train yourself to think that water is really the only beverage you should drink. Avoid sugary, caffeinated, and carbonated beverages altogether, and drink water with meals. You should also not wait until you feel thirsty to drink water, as this indicates that your body is already low on fluids. Drinking plenty of water will help your body thrive during astral projection!

If drinking solely water is not your thing, you are welcome to add tea to your menu. White tea is your best bet because it is the least processed and retains the most natural benefits—followed by green and black teas. Tea has antioxidants, may decrease your risk of having a stroke or heart attack, and it is good for both your immune and digestive systems. It is also hot and soothing, which can do wonders for our comfort. There is a reason that the British have long been known for sitting down with 'a cuppa' at times of stress and trouble.

Meditate

There are numerous proven benefits to meditation, and it can be an extremely useful tool in astral projection. Some of the best reasons to meditate are stress reduction, increased compassion, greater concentration and awareness, and an increased sense of calmness and self. All of these will help you have a successful astral projection. With meditation, you are training your brain to consciously relax and ignore distractions. For people just beginning meditation, it is recommended to find a guided meditation that you like, as having expert instruction can be an invaluable teaching technique. There are countless options online, so you can try as many as you like. It might take you a while to find a good one; it is important to be patient and give yourself over to the experience. In the end, the benefits will outweigh the frustrations!

It is also a great idea to practice meditation on your own. One popular beginning meditation method is known as the 4-7-8 Breathing Technique. It is very simple and straightforward. To begin, sit in a quiet location, anywhere where you won't be disturbed. You can sit on a chair or on the floor, possibly with some pillows for comfort. Sit up straight, close your eyes and breathe in through your nose for four counts. You hold your breath for seven counts, then exhale through your mouth for eight counts. Pay attention to how your body feels, how you can feel the air moving in and out of your lungs. Think of inhaling the good and exhaling the bad. You will feel yourself relax as your mind clears—this is where you want to be! If you feel your mind start to wander, always return to the 4-7-8 count, as concentrating on this will help keep you from getting distracted. Practicing meditation is an ideal preparation for astral projection. You will learn to focus and concentrate while also relaxing and entering a clear state of being.

Another beginning technique for meditation involves simply concentrating on a specific thing--anything the practitioner chooses. You can repeat a word or mantra in your mind, follow your breathing, or listen to white noise in the background. This should be anything that allows you to focus on the act of meditation, and that you can quickly return to if you find your thoughts wandering.

Visualize

You also want to spend time visualizing yourself in the astral realm. This is just what it sounds like—practice seeing yourself apart from your body. This will allow you to gain more control and confidence when you are actually experiencing astral projection and will make the transition much smoother.

Obstacles

The fact that you are interested in and preparing for astral projection indicates that you are open to the experience and have a good chance of success. There are, however, obstacles that may stand in your way.

Fear

The idea of undertaking astral projection sounds scary. There is so much that is unknown about the astral plane. Even if you feel that you already know a lot about it and have spoken to numerous people about their experiences, it is not the same thing as experiencing it firsthand. Every person's experience will be different, and there is a great deal of the unfamiliar in this realm. That is part of what makes astral projection so intriguing, but it also makes it frightening. To combat feelings of fear, it is recommended that you give yourself plenty of time to prepare. It is understandable that you are excited and can't wait to get started, but it makes sense to do everything you can beforehand to ensure your success. Again, meditation is an incredible resource that will work wonders in preparing you for your journey. Give yourself five minutes here or there, whenever you can, do focus your mind and give yourself confidence. As you train your mind, you will gain mental strength and more control over yourself. It is quite similar to an athlete in training, and you can think of your preparation in this way. You will see the benefits as you prepare in a smart, attentive manner. You may even be surprised by feeling better, stronger and more confident in your daily life and interactions with others.

Doubt

What if astral projection isn't real? Regardless of how deeply you may believe in it, it is more than understandable if you still wonder if there is anything there. You don't want to invest the time in research and preparation only to end up feeling disappointed and foolish.

It is impossible to guarantee that any person will be able to enter the astral realm. The thing to remember is that it is really up to you to have a successful astral projection. Every person is capable of it, but only through preparation, research and belief will it actually happen. Remember this, and you will be able to quell the doubt. You must remain open-minded and believe in what you're doing. Doubt may do its best to slow you down or even stop you but remember that your passion is stronger than the doubt.

Also remember that even if your astral projection doesn't look or feel like you thought it would, that doesn't mean it was a failure! Try appreciating the experience for what it was, be grateful for it, and look forward to doing it again. Attitude is everything!

Chapter 3: Best Astral Projection Techniques and How to Perform Them

All of these techniques will allow you to pursue astral projection, but they may take time! Do not get discouraged if you find yourself thinking about other things—just refocus back to the task at hand. As with anything else, all of these take practice, dedication, and diligence. The reward will be there, however, when you achieve your goal and accomplish astral projection. Just remember to be patient. Whether it takes minutes or days, you will get there!

Space

Make sure that you are in a location that will be absolutely free from distractions. There can't be anyone speaking in the background. no cell phones, TVs, or music playing. no pets trying to get your attention--nothing. These normal, everyday background noises will keep you from focusing on freeing your astral body and will guarantee that you are unable to obtain your goals. No matter what it takes, you must ensure that your environment is conducive to a peaceful, spiritual undertaking. Maybe you send everyone in your home off to the movies for a couple of hours, power down your electronics, and take this time for yourself. Not only will your astral projection be enhanced, but you will find that the simple act of taking care of yourself will give you benefits in your everyday life. Self-care is an important key to spiritual development and living a happy life.

You will also want to decorate your setting to make it conducive to relaxation and free from negativity. Having some healthy, green leafy plants around will help clean the air, create a feeling of peace, and overall enrich your environment. Some plants that are known for attracting positive energy are rosemary, jasmine, Aloe Vera, and orchid—among others. Having fresh flowers in your space will also add to the positive vibrations. Burning incense can be a great trick to lead your mood in a certain direction. You can also use essential oils in a diffuser to create a positive disposition in your environment. The best scents to encourage relaxation, brain function, and positivity are lavender, cinnamon, valerian, vanilla, pine, and jasmine. You will be surprised at how inhaling these fragrances will help you relax and focus on the exciting adventure you are undertaking.

Depending on how deep your interest goes, you can incorporate the practice of Feng Shui to attract positive energy into your home. This is a practice that allows you to achieve balance while maximizing your likely attainment of success—all by adjusting your living space. For example, doors and windows should not be blocked by furniture in order to encourage free, unimpeded flow of energy between rooms. Also, the placement of light fixtures can impact balance and support, and mirrors can be used to optimize energy. Candles are also a great accessory and are much more calming than bright, overhead lights. The gentle, flickering light makes a great background to the meditating and spiritual travel that you are doing. It encourages the dreamy, softly defined atmosphere we need. You can definitely use scented candles in the same fragrances described above. However, it is recommended that you only use one scented accessory at a time—so don't combine candles, incense, essential oils, and/or anything else. It will smell overwhelmingly strong and probably distract you, thereby interfering with your astral journey.

Healing crystals are a great addition to your spiritual arsenal. They contain powers connected to thousands of years of the history of the Earth, all there to help you attach to higher forces. Crystals emanate beautiful, peaceful forces that will really help you rise to a higher plane. You can use them as decorations in your space to remind you to concentrate and focus on your vibrational state. Carry them with you to serve as a talisman, giving you something to focus on, no matter where you are. You can even hold crystals in your hands during meditation and use them to assist with focusing and breathing. The study of healing crystals is fascinating and complex, and it will add a lot to your spiritual practice if you choose to include it.

Breathe

Focus on your breathing. Don't allow your mind to wander--if you catch it, go right back to your breathing. Paying attention to your breathing is often difficult for people to master, accustomed as we are to daily distractions and multitasking. Think 'breathe in' as you inhale and 'breathe out' as you exhale; this will help you stay focused on your breaths. Some people also like to count each breath as they take it. Focus on your breaths filling and relaxing your body. You need your body to begin feeling extremely relaxed and almost disconnected. You should also practice mindful breathing for 15-minute periods every day. It may sound like you will need to dedicate a lot of time to astral projection and its associated acts but know that these can easily be woven into your daily life. They can even be combined so that obviously you are breathing while you are doing everything else—you wouldn't be alive, otherwise! This is just a recommendation to add mindfulness everywhere, including to the simple, automatic act of breathing.

Meditate

This is a very important portion of astral projection, as was noted previously. Without being able to properly meditate and move to a deeper state of consciousness, it is possible that your attempts will fail. Not only is meditation hugely important to relaxation, but it also helps prepare the body and mind for the upcoming separation. This is naturally stressful, especially when you're new to astral projection, and the stress and fear can get in the way and prevent a successful experience.

It is worthwhile to briefly introduce the idea of chakras, which we will return to later in this book. There are seven chakras, or energy centers, in the body. They are Root, Sacral, Solar Plexus, Heart, Throat, Third Eye and Crown. If the energy centers become clogged due to negative vibrational activity, it can stunt your spiritual growth and ability to enter the astral realm or cause you to have a less than positive experience when you are there. One way to help clear out the chakras is to meditate on color, as each chakra has a color associated with it. Spend up to five or ten breaths thinking about these colors, and you will be taking great steps to positively increase your body's energy flow.

The colors are in the same order as the rainbow beginning with red and following the spectrum through to purple. First is red in the Root chakra, associated with ground and earth. Next is orange for Sacral, creativity, and desire; yellow for Solar Plexus, obviously the sun; green for the Heart, again for the Earth, all living things, especially those that grow from the land. Next up is light blue for the Throat chakra, it refers to sound; indigo for the Third Eye and light; and finally, purple for the Crown chakra and the light of truth.

At this point, you will be approaching the line between consciousness and unconsciousness. This is also known as a hypnagogic state, meaning just between being awake and being asleep. You may feel as though you have been hypnotized, while some people say it feels like dreaming. The difference to keep in mind, however, is that you are in control of what happens to you here! People who are hypnotized or dreaming are neither awake nor in command of their thoughts and actions. Astral projection is a *willful* undertaking, and that is what you need to remember any time you find yourself feeling unsure or afraid. You are awake, you want to be here, and you are guiding yourself through the process. Thanks to meditation and breathing, you are calm, focused and prepared for the next step in the process.

Vibrational Stage

Now, once you are well into deep breathing and meditation, you should feel your consciousness begin to alter and may literally feel that your body is vibrating or moving in some way. This is called the 'vibrational stage,' as practitioners believe that what you are feeling are the actual vibrations of your soul. This can be an intense feeling, especially if you're new to astral projection, so it is important to stay calm, continue breathing and keep your mind clear. Nothing bad is happening to you! Just remember that you want to feel the vibrations, as that feeling means your journey in astral projection is successful and you are beginning to separate from your body. Continue with breathing and meditation and stay relaxed! You should soon start to enjoy and appreciate the vibrations, and it should be a pleasurable experience. It is also a sure sign that your spiritual energy is strong.

It is possible to raise your vibrational frequency and increase that connection to the spiritual world. This is definitely something that is in our best interest, and fortunately the best techniques that we are implementing due to our increased spiritual activity. For starters, make sure that you are breathing mindfully. This helps to begin the adjustment. Take some time to take a break and give yourself some care. Really think about your feelings, as ignoring them can lead to spiritual blockages that can impede your progress. This is not a time for you to beat down or ignore your feelings. Especially if you are going through a lot in your life (and really, who isn't?), it is crucial that you address and deal with your feelings as they occur. Only by being honest with ourselves can we have any hope of obtaining spiritual growth and being better, happier people. Finally, repeat a mantra to help you cultivate love and compassion. Following these tips will allow us to begin lifting our vibrational frequency, further expanding our consciousness and allowing us a better connection with the spiritual world.

If you choose to devote some extra time to increase your vibrational frequency in order to give you greater access to the astral plane, there are some practices you can follow. Since every person is made up of four energy levels (physical, mental, emotional and spiritual), each of which needs to have positive vibrational flow, it makes sense to take care of them. Much of this is covered elsewhere in this book because it is good advice and is proven to work. Surround yourself with optimistic, happy people. Like attracts like, so you want to have as much good energy around you as possible. Eat a healthy balanced diet, be conscious of your thoughts and the world around you, meditate, be kind and grateful. And, it is really a great idea to exercise and get your body moving. A healthy body is a happy body, and your vibrational energy will respond well to increased oxygen levels. You will also have more power in your physical life and will find yourself moving purposefully and confidently through your days.

Visualize Movement

At this point in astral projection, you will remain absolutely still while visualizing, or imagining, yourself moving. It is important to remember that the movement here is not in the physical world. Some people recommend visualizing small, repetitive movements, such as flexing your arm or bending over to touch your toes. Really allow yourself to focus on the details of what you are 'seeing' and 'doing.' Notice the feeling of air flowing against your arm as you raise it back to a 90-degree angle, or the slight head rush you feel as you fold your body forward to the ground. The point is to make the visualization as realistic as possible.

Once you master small movements, you are ready to move on to larger visualized actions. These can include seeing yourself flying through the air or shooting out of a cannon--even picturing yourself literally pulling yourself out of your physical body by climbing a rope. Again, it is crucial to be mindful of what you are seeing. Instead of just noting that you are flying, pay attention to how the world looks from your higher elevation and how your body feels, in addition to any other sensations you may notice. Look down and see yourself lying in the deeply relaxed state while you are above. You must work to keep your mind active and engaged in the process, or you run the risk of simply falling asleep and missing out on the astral projection experience.

It has been shown that visualization is an important tool for personal development, not just in the astral realm, but in the physical world. It can help you achieve goals and live the life you want, one that you are excited about and proud of. Not only can you do it internally, but you can create a vision (or dream) board to help you manifest and attract what you want. These can be a lot of fun and a great creative outlet. Stimulating your creative side can also help inspire your vibrational frequency. Isn't it fascinating how interconnected everything is?

Astral Projection

You are now ready to begin astral projection! To do this, you need to separate your astral body from your physical body. This is fairly straightforward but requires all of your concentration and faith as well as your mind to do so. You should use whatever format works for you. Some people remove one part at a time, starting with their toes and working their way up the body. Others visualize themselves pulling up on a rope hanging overhead; some see themselves shooting out of a cannon into the astral realm. It is most important that you believe in whatever method you choose—otherwise, you are almost guaranteed to fail. For beginners, it is strongly recommended that they choose a slow and deliberate method of removal so that the transition is as gentle and free from fear as possible.

A popular technique for astral projection is known as the Monroe Steps. It includes seven easy-to-follow steps that will guide your astral body to leave your physical self. The seven steps are:

1. First, simply relax your body and mind.
2. Relax into the trancelike state of "hypnagogia" (somewhere between sleeping and wakefulness).
3. Encourage, within yourself, the feelings of mental strength and control, rather than feelings from the physical self; engage with your astral self.
4. Be aware of the spiritual plane vibrating all around you; it feels welcoming rather than threatening.
5. Enter and embrace the vibrational state; your astral body is preparing to join the astral plane.
6. Concentrate on exiting from the physical body into the astral realm, slowly and with intention; you will pull your spiritual self, part by part, from your physical self.
7. Conclude the process by guiding your astral self out of the body. Just visualize yourself separating, and it will be so.

Once your astral body is separated from your physical body, you should take a few minutes to simply appreciate what you've accomplished. Look at your physical body in repose, where you left it in the physical world, as your astral body hovers above it in a different dimension of time and space. It is really remarkable that you've been able to achieve as much as you have already, as many people aren't equipped to venture this far into the spiritual world. This will also allow you to become comfortable being separate from your physical body. Know that your physical body is completely safe and at peace while you are conducting your spiritual journey. You are still breathing, blood is flowing, you are ALIVE! Although people who experience astral projection almost uniformly report a positive experience, it can still be overwhelming. You should allow yourself as much time as you need to adjust to this new state of being. It is more likely, however, that you will feel good and be too excited to hang around your physical body for long. You have successfully achieved your goal; now is the time to reap the rewards!

At all times, you should be focused on your lucidity. You can't let yourself fall asleep, no matter how perfectly relaxed you may feel. If you are aware you are lucid, this allows you to remain in control of your experience, will increase your enjoyment and help raise your consciousness even further. If you do fall asleep, you will likely begin having a lucid dream, which means basically that you are aware that you are dreaming. You cannot control your actions in the dreams (or the dreams themselves), so that is a different experience than astral projection.

It is important to note here that you don't need to worry about becoming permanently separated from your physical body. There is a strong, psychic connection linking the astral body to the physical one. Some people refer to it as a 'silver cord.' It is infinitely long and flexible, allowing the practitioner to travel as far and wide as he desires. But it is also absolutely unbreakable and serves as a permanent conductor back to the body. This knowledge will hopefully give you even more confidence and sense of adventure during astral projection, as it is a virtual guarantee of success! Think of it as a perfect, spiritual umbilical cord. It gives you ultimate freedom along with ultimate safety.

Now, you are officially in the astral realm!

For first timers, it is highly recommended that you stay within the confines of your home. Start out by wandering around whatever room you are in, noticing as many details as you can. Those details may not exactly correspond to what is there in reality, but this is unimportant, as you are experiencing a completely different realm than what you are used to. Then begin moving from room to room, exploring to your heart's content. While this is considered a beginners' practice, it should be noted that this is still happening in the astral realm. That is an astounding statement and will hopefully keep beginners from feeling that they have to go too far, too fast. Keep it nice and slow for the first time and be grateful for what you are experiencing.

You will probably feel like you are weightless, you will feel dreamy yet very aware, and it is possible that you will feel somewhat unsteady. This is absolutely normal and to be expected. As you become more experienced, these feelings will lessen, and you will become more surefooted and certain in how you can get around. Again, giving yourself time to master your place in the astral world can and should be fun. Here you can walk through walls, float as if weightless, move through different dimensions... the list is endless.

As you continue with astral projection, you will find that there really are no limits. You can explore the farthest ranges of outer space, every astrological wonder, solar system, black hole, all of it. You can travel through all of time, from the Big Bang, through all of the different periods to the beginning of human existence. Experience (for 'real!') ancient Greece, the Renaissance, the Revolutionary War, anything and everything up to modern times. Literally, nothing is off limits or out of reach. You will encounter an infinite variety of other beings, some familiar, some utterly unfamiliar. Most amazingly, you will meet other people, just like you, who are tourists in the astral plane. You can actually make new friends and travel companions—just in a different realm than the usual one!

You can visit different civilizations and societies, multiverses, every part of planet Earth (from the depths of the seas to the highest mountain peaks), and who knows what else! That is one of the best and most exciting parts of this--that there is so much that is unknown but just waiting to be discovered. Shrink down to microscopic size and explore the inside of the human body, see what it is really like inside a beehive, or be the proverbial 'fly on the wall' during mankind's most well-known moments of the past! You can meet famous, historical figures, contact your own departed loved ones, and interact with creatures from different species. Why not take to the skies in hot-air balloons, dive to mysterious ocean depths and cross the Arctic on foot.

Another possible idea when learning about astral projection is to learn more about the Buddhist religion. Buddhism and astral projection are both strongly focused on increased consciousness. There is a word in Sanskrit, 'vijnana,' that means 'life force' or 'consciousness.' This word is found throughout Buddhist literature and is dissected through numerous levels of conscious states. There is a strong mind-body connection in Buddhism, which also connects it to the astral realm. It is an interesting religion that has a sense of spirituality to it. It is certainly not required that any religious faith need be involved in the study of astral projection, but it can definitely be one consideration out of many. It is just another tool in your toolkit for spiritual growth.

No matter how you approach astral projection or what you hope to get out of it, you can really go as far as you want to with it. You can master all of the techniques listed here and become advanced in your practice. Maybe you will feel such a strong connection that you begin teaching classes and guiding people through their own astral projections. You will definitely learn new and unexpected things about yourself and the universe, and it makes sense that you will want to share this knowledge with others that you care about. There are so many ways that you can do this. If you feel like it, you can invite people to know more about astral projection with you. Or you may want to go in a more generally spiritual direction. Maybe you want to start a meditation, Tai Chi or yoga class at work during lunchtime for your coworkers. This can be a fun and non-threatening way to share some quiet, meditative time without getting too deeply into the spiritual side of things. It is really a good idea from a health and wellness point of view. Many workplaces will provide space for a workout or activity such as this, and study after study has shown that healthy, well-balanced employees are more productive. That, of course, means it is in the company's best interest to allow and encourage these activities. It is also a great way for you to stay connected to the spiritual side of things even when you are away from home. Just because you aren't enjoying a quiet bath or resting in your quiet meditative space at home, does not mean that you should completely forget about raising your consciousness when you are out in the physical world. You can deepen your friendships and make new ones, all while helping these people and yourself keep your chakras clear and flowing smoothly, raising your consciousness, and practicing self-care. Many of the techniques here work well as bonding exercises with other people.

It can also be a great idea to involve your children, if you have any, in spiritual growth and development. Young people are naturally more open-minded and less cynical than adults and are therefore normally more able to access their mystical sides. Set aside time to practice meditation with your children, take a parent and child yoga class--any number of things are possible. Again, this is both extremely useful for you and your child's spiritual growth. It is also a great way to bond with your child while enjoying a fun activity. Your child will probably take to the new, spiritual pursuit right away, with a child's sense of wonder and achievement. This can lead children to become incredibly developed and knowledgeable, compassionate and empathetic. Children who are able to grow up in this spiritually-aware manner will become kind and grateful adults, who are connected to the world and want to make it a better place. In the long run, that will only benefit all of mankind and the planet we live on. And there really is no better time to start than now.

Chapter 4: How Do I Come Back and What to Do After?

All good things must come to an end—unfortunately, that also includes astral projection. At some point, you will have to return to your physical body in this world and resume your normal life. You should return to an overwhelming sensation of peace, love, and raised consciousness. You may also feel tired, overwhelmed, and needing time to process your feelings about what you've just experienced. All of this is completely normal and understandable. You have just lived through something that—while all of us can do it—not all of us will. It can be a lot for some people to deal with. What you have done is really special.

To return to your physical body, you need to remember the silver cord that we spoke of earlier—the umbilical cord connecting the astral and the physical. It will now guide you back home, allowing you to reconnect your astral body with your soul. As with other aspects of astral projection, this purposeful relinking will be very positive and uplifting.

As we mentioned before, the silver cord is infinitely stretchable and completely unbreakable. It can never be torn, cut, tangled, or in any way removed. It will always, always, *always* connect the astral body and the physical body. Hence, just as they 'follow the yellow brick road' in the Wizard of Oz, you will follow the silver cord to get you back home. It really is as easy as that. Wherever you are in the astral realm, whoever you are with, whatever you are doing, your silver cord will be there—acting as the liaison between you in the spiritual world and your physical body.

So, once it is time to return to your physical body and end astral projection, all you have to do is grab hold of your silver cord and take yourself home. It can happen instantaneously, if you so desire. Concepts of distance, time, etc. are meaningless and have no bearing in the spiritual realm. As with the rest of your travels, you can decide how you want to get back. You can snap your fingers and—voila—you are back in your physical body. Maybe you want to see yourself following the silver cord like a guide rope or following a path of breadcrumbs. You can fly, take a hot air balloon, shoot from a cannon—however you feel most comfortable is the best method for your return journey. Just guide yourself and make it happen.

It is also a really good idea to set a timer of some sort to remind you when it is time to end your astral projection session. As people get more and more involved with this practice, it can become easy to lose track of time—especially since time, space, and matter are irrelevant in the spiritual realm. Time spent outside your body can seem like minutes but really be hours or vice versa. It is also, of course, critical to not spend all of your time astral projecting! You need time to sleep, rejuvenate, and simply live your physical life—eating, working, exercising, playing, etc. Setting a soft, gentle timer to alert you that it is time to take hold of the silver cord and begin to follow it home will be most helpful. It is also understandable if you put the timer on sleep when it first alerts you—take the final few minutes to complete your project, conversation, or journey that you are experiencing and then follow the silver cord home to your physical body. It should not be loud and jarring, like an alarm clock, but something like chanting, rhythmic gongs, or soft music—

anything that can grab your attention in the astral world without disrupting your journey.

It is most likely that you will regain full consciousness when you are back in your physical body. It is not technically waking up, of course, because you are not asleep, but that is the easiest description of how the sensation of returning feels. It is different from leaving, which requires more effort on your part. Coming back is much simpler and more rapid. All of a sudden, you are back where you started.

Now it is important to perform a system check on yourself and see how you are feeling. It is highly likely that, in the beginning, you will be both invigorated and slightly dazed. Invigorated because you just achieved a goal that is truly spectacular and unique. Dazed for those same reasons—it can be a lot for any person to process. Your body may also be feeling slightly stiff or unused, depending on how long your projection has been. Take a few minutes to familiarize yourself with how it feels to be back, reacquainting yourself with your body and the physical world. Embrace the feelings that have returned with you from the astral world. You should retain the sensations of raised consciousness, love and peace, which is, for many people, the reason for beginning astral projection in the first place.

You can stay here for a few minutes to ease your journey back to the physical world. Focus on your breathing (practice the 4-7-8 technique), repeat your mantras, and stay relaxed. You want to hold on to the positive feelings that you brought back, as this will really make a difference in your everyday life in the physical world. A good mantra here might be something simple like 'I will remember,' which will help tell your brain that you want to retain this information. Really pay attention as you repeat the phrase.

Many practitioners find it fun and helpful to keep an astral projection journal. Journaling is receiving increased recognition for its benefits, such as increasing mindfulness, improving memory and comprehension, and encouraging more self-discipline. Journaling after astral projection offers all of these benefits, along with the vitally important function of helping you to remember and process what you experienced in the spiritual realm. You also don't have to worry about hoping you remember everything, as you are creating a record that you can refer back to whenever you choose.

On a more technical note, when you are in the astral realm, your experiences are happening to your 'extra-physical' brain. The ideas here are to transfer your experience from there to your physical brain. As you continue with astral projection, you will constantly build upon your current knowledge, ever raising your consciousness to even higher levels. It is almost like making a New Year's resolution, except even better. It is more likely that you will hold on to the lessons, especially since you can astral project as often as you like—not once a year like New Year's!

Your spiritual growth will be remarkably accelerated by the transfer of energy from the astral world to this one. There are no limits there, so your consciousness can rise to ever greater heights by your journeys. This is very exciting and transformative—it should be something that you will really enjoy. You will see the benefits in all areas of your life—other relationships, in your job, your overall level of happiness and enjoyment of life. The possibilities are endless, just like the limits of what you can achieve through astral projection. You are not even limited by your own imagination, and without these restrictions, it can certainly make a tremendous difference.

Chapter 5: What Is the Downside of Astral Projection?

So many parts of astral projection are not only positive but are really special and it can be easy to think that there are no drawbacks whatsoever. As with anything else, however, there are going to be aspects of this that are less positive than others. Fortunately, these are all within our control, and we can make sure to work toward constructive solutions.

One is that you may become too involved with your interest in the astral plane. There is so much about spiritual travel that is truly wonderful and better than life in the physical realm that you may be tempted to spend an inordinate amount of time journeying. This is clearly unhealthy and should be avoided. You must always focus your time and energy on the physical realm. No matter how much 'better' the astral world may seem, the physical world is our reality. Life here must be embraced and lived, not seen only as time spent between astral journeys. Any sort of obsession is bad, and too much of an interest in astral projection is no different. Don't neglect other parts of your life.

Another potential downside is that you may focus on your relationships with other devotees of astral travel, often online, to the detriment of relationships with the people in your real world. While online relationships with fellow enthusiasts of astral projection can be very important and rewarding, they are only one part of a healthy, well-rounded life, and should not be focused on exclusively. Make sure to spend time with friends and family. Go outside, partake in hobbies and other enjoyments. Travel and experience life. While astral projection can be an important part of your spiritual journey and life in general, it should complement your life, not overwhelm it.

Unfortunately, some people in your life will not be supportive of your interest in the spiritual world. Some people might even make fun of it and be downright insulting. It can be terribly difficult to maintain positive relationships with people like this, regardless of how long you have known them and how important the relationship is. Who knows what the motivation is for disparaging something that means so much to someone else, but that doesn't really matter as far as you are concerned. It will probably be easier to just not talk about your interest in astral projection, even though you may feel this is unfair. Why should you be held back in sharing something you are passionate about, just because of someone else's negativity? That is a decision you will have to make yourself. Can you keep someone in your life who makes you feel this way? Ironically, your spiritual growth may be the thing that enables you to work through these feelings. You will be developing increased compassion and empathy, which are the very characteristics that allow you to deal with difficult people in your life. It is very possible for you to rise above this obstacle, treat these people with loving kindness, and continue to pursue astral projection. Or you may decide that it just isn't worth it to be around negativity and that it encourages self-doubt. In that case, you should remove that person from your life, recognizing that this will probably be painful.

Religious beliefs can stand in the way of successful astral projection as it can be difficult to reconcile faith and an interest in the paranormal. Open-mindedness is the most important balance to this knowledge. It is possible for a person to be religious and a traveler in the spiritual realm, if they so desire. As long as the person is honest with himself and open about what these different aspects of life and growth mean, there is definitely room for both sets of beliefs in a balanced life. There may be some indication that some aspects of out-of-body experiences are referenced in religious traditions including Buddhism and some Biblical interpretations. That could be a comfort for people looking to reconcile two things that seem so different.

It is worth remembering here that you cannot become lost in the spiritual world, you cannot be injured or sick, you cannot hurt anyone, and you cannot have any impact on events or people in the physical world. In other words, what happens in the astral realm, stays in the astral realm!

It is wondered if you can be possessed by a demon or be hurt by some kind of negative spirit. No, you do not have to worry about a devil taking over your body and making you do awful things under its influence. As for the other, it is possible that you will run into beings or spirits that do not have positive intentions. While you may encounter them, they will not have any power to influence you or your actions because you are in control of what you do. If you intended to go into the astral realm with negative intentions, it wouldn't work anyway.

Some people have repeated difficulty in staying in a hypnagogic state. They find themselves so relaxed that they fall asleep. The experience then moves into the realm of lucid dreaming, rather than astral projection.

Lucid dreaming is an interesting concept that can and should be explored by those with an interest in the paranormal. When you are lucid dreaming, you are asleep but aware that you are dreaming. If you find yourself moving between astral projection and lucid dreaming, you should embrace both experiences. One benefit of lucid dreaming is that you can refer to a number of dream interpretations that can help you explain what you are experiencing in your dreams and what it means in your real life. There is no similar interpreter for astral projection, so this is something working in lucid dreaming's favor.

While astral projection is great and the majority of the people you meet are as well, you need to be aware that you run the risk of being scammed. Since there is nor can there be any sort of proof or evidence, unscrupulous people can try to take advantage for financial gain. They can claim to be a guide to the astral realm, can offer products or services, and can serve as a communication link with people on the other side. Some people can offer this knowledge, while others only see the opportunity to make a quick buck. The best and most effective way to make sure that people claiming to be spiritually enlightened are legitimate is to do research. You can search for them online, talk to other people and friends and see what kind of chemistry you have with these people. Often, your own sixth sense is a great indicator of whether something is legitimate or whether it is sketchy. Also, pay attention to online reviews and what people are saying. If the overall perception seems to be that these spiritual experts don't deliver on what they promise, trust what the reviewers say unless it seems like the reviews have an ax to grind or some interest other than honesty and community service. Online evaluations are a great way to find out the truth and whether or not guides can actually give you the guidance and expertise that they promise.

The main risk of astral projection is simply fear of the unknown. Once those fears are faced and addressed, we gain control over them and they dissipate. Meditation, breathing, mantras, visualization--all of these techniques make for a smooth preparation, entrance, journey and return.

Chapter 6: Frequently Asked Questions About Astral Projection

How Much Time Does It Take to Astral Project?

While some people do experience impulsive or involuntary out-of-body experiences, for most people, it will take some time to achieve the journey. Whether that is due to heightened spiritual function or some other explanation does not really matter. As we have discussed, it is smart to take some time and prepare for traveling to the astral realm. There is no set guide, however, for how much time you should invest in the preparation, the journey and reentry, and the recovery.

Everyone has a completely unique adventure with astral projection, and this includes the amount of time invested. You may be so excited and enthusiastic that you decide to get started with only a few hours of preparation. Others may take a more cautious approach and spend more time with research and talking to other people before getting started. However, as much time as you need to make you feel the most comfortable and secure is how much time you should spend preparing.

As for how much time the astral projection itself takes, the answer should probably be under 30 minutes for beginners. That is enough time to meditate into the vibrational state, separate from the physical body, enter and travel through the astral plane, and return. Also, remember that 30 minutes in Earth time can be an unlimited time in the spiritual realm. You won't ever feel rushed or as though you don't have enough time to do everything you want to do. Remember to set a timer to remind you to end your travels and come back to real life. As you continue to develop, you may find it will take more or less time, and you can adjust your schedule accordingly.

Do I Need to Protect Myself in Any Way?

There is really nothing to fear in the astral plane or your journeys there, so we would recommend preparing yourself through all of the techniques named here, and don't worry about protecting yourself. You will be just great.

How Do I Know If It Worked?

There is no checklist that you can run through to determine if you achieved a spiritual journey. What you can do, though, is sit back and relax, relive your experience, and see how you feel about it. One of the main determinants of success is how positively you feel about the occurrence. In other words, if you feel that you successfully traveled to the astral realm and accomplished what you hoped, then you should consider that a win!

You can feel good about your travels if you achieved the vibrational state and feel connected to the spiritual world. Maybe you even feel that you were able to raise your consciousness. The vibrational state is an especially good measure, as it indicates increased levels of consciousness and something that just does not happen during the course of normal, daily life. You will feel your spiritual energy as it courses through your body, and it should feel stronger and more present than normal. Since you just spent some time in the astral plane, it only makes sense that your spiritual forces are enhanced.

This will be a tremendous feeling that hopefully, you can build upon and that will stay with you as you go through your day.

Am I Crazy to Believe in Astral Projection?

In a word—no.

There is so much in this world and human experience that seems unexplainable by 'rational' means. It has made sense to millions of people since the beginning of time to investigate the spiritual realm for personal growth and to learn more about what it means to be human. While traveling out-of-body has not been scientifically proven, and there is much about it that is not described, it is very real for the people who believe in it. Especially considering that there really are no downsides to traveling through the astral realm. It is one of the only truly positive experiences that we can have. More and more people all the time are expressing an interest in the spiritual world and finding a growing community of like-minded individuals should be a very positive thing in your life.

I Haven't Been Able to Achieve Astral Projection—What Can I Do?

It is possible that you are overthinking the issue and trying too hard. You may be so obsessed with experiencing the spiritual world that you are unable to achieve your goal. Try relaxing in a dark, quiet room and just breathing. Let go of everything else and just breathe. This will help keep you focused and calm. It is very possible that just by clearing away all distractions and focusing on the breath, you may be able to achieve the hypnagogic state and then the astral plane.

If you are interested in a greater spiritual experience, you may want to investigate clearing your chakras. The chakras are the energy center of the body and act as mystical fuel to the astral body. They can become blocked for a number of reasons, including past trauma or self-doubt. Clearing chakras can be very healing and cathartic—

and of course, the benefits will extend to both the physical and astral worlds.

To clear your chakras, it is recommended that you:

- Spend time in nature, enjoying yourself at the ocean, mountains, or by a river. It may even just mean taking a walk outside if that is all that is available to you. Sunshine and fresh air are notoriously powerful healers.
- Take a hot, cleansing bath.
- Get up early and spend some quiet time before the craziness of the day begins.
- Try doing yoga, as it is known for its focus on centering.
- If you can, spend time with a pet. Bonding with a furry friend can be a great stress reducer.
- Write in a journal about what stresses you are experiencing, as well as good things that are happening.
- Meditate and focus on raising your consciousness. Spend time doing quick five-minute meditations whenever you have the time and space. Also follow longer, guided meditations that specifically focus on positive energy flow and clearing your chakras.

Following these suggestions will help clear out and balance your chakras. Once your chakras are in a better state, your energy force will flow freely and a major source of resistance to astral projection will be removed.

Is It Possible to Switch Bodies with Someone Else?

No, this is not something that we are familiar with ever having happened. It sounds as it would be impossible—since the object of astral traveling is that you remain in control of yourself the whole time.

Are There Any Drugs or Substances I Can Take to Help with Astral Projection?

It is not recommended that you use mind-altering materials to travel through the spiritual realm. While there are some hallucinogenic and other types of drugs that seem to offer similar experiences, you need to be in control of yourself in order to astral project. By the very act of taking drugs, you are by definition giving up your self-control. How will you know if your excursion was a true journey through the spiritual world or just a trip? Illicit substances may act to block your chakras further complicating the issue. Taking drugs, even if it is meant to heighten your astral experience, really negates the entire operation and should be avoided.

Are Near-Death Experiences a Type of Astral Projection?

Yes. The difference between astral projection and a near-death experience is that the former is voluntary, and the latter is not. People undertake astral projection for spiritual growth and fun. During a near death experience, a person is actually in the process of dying. The spirit, which is the life force, separates from the body and crosses over, starting the trip from life to death. It often involves traversing a long hallway toward a white light, which is understood to be the place where death occurs. They may even see their life passing before their eyes, taking stock before the end. The person's life is saved, and he returns from the astral world to his physical body. During a near-death experience, the person is not in control of his experience.

When Is the Best Time to Astral Project?

It is most important not to astral project at night or too close to your bedtime. There is just too much risk that you will fall asleep and miss out on the experience. While it seems logical that it would be easiest right before bed, evidence shows that is not the case. Many people report that it is the easiest first thing in the morning, perhaps because that is the closest to the hypnagogic state and because you're still waking up. That is not feasible for everyone, though, whether due to family or work commitments, so it is up to your individual preferences. Pretty much anytime you have the time and physical space available for astral projection is the best option for you. Whether that is supported or criticized by anyone else is irrelevant.

Conclusion

Thank you for making it through to the end of *Astral Projection: Unlocking the Secrets of Astral Travel and Having a Willful Out-of-Body Experience, Including Tips for Entering the Astral Plane and Shifting into Higher Consciousness*! Let's hope it was informative and able to provide you with all of the tools you need to achieve your goals, whatever they may be.

The next step is to get busy with astral projection! There is no reason to wait as you can begin working on your spiritual self immediately. Work on your vibrational energy and raising your consciousness. Start by slowing down, breathing mindfully, and setting up a meditation space. If you are really serious and excited to explore, you can start your journey into the astral world as soon as tonight. As we noted, however, it does not hurt to stop and take your time preparing. The more knowledge and self-awareness you bring to astral projection, the more confident you will be, and your experience will be more successful as a result.

Also included in this tome are some different self-care techniques. These will offer benefits in the astral realm as well as in the physical realm. Your life can be enhanced in so many different ways. You can really start to live the life you want. The sky (and beyond) is the limit—don't stop once you get started!

Finally, if you found this book useful in any way, a review on Amazon is always appreciated!

Printed in Great Britain
by Amazon